D0062118

**Showdown**

# Animal Defenses

**Jennifer Kroll**

## Publishing Credits

Rachelle Cracchiolo, M.S.Ed., *Publisher*
Conni Medina, M.A.Ed., *Managing Editor*
Nika Fabienke, Ed.D., *Series Developer*
June Kikuchi, *Content Director*
John Leach, *Assistant Editor*
Kevin Pham, *Graphic Designer*

TIME For Kids and the TIME For Kids logo are registered trademarks of TIME Inc. Used under license.

**Image Credits:** Cover and p.1 _548901005677/Getty Images; pp.4–5 Roy Toft/National Geographic Creative; p.18 INTERFOTO/Alamy Stock Photo; p.19 (top) Universal Images Group North America LLC/Alamy Stock Photo; p.24 Michel Gunther/Science Source; p.25 John Serrao/Science Source; all other images from iStock and/or Shutterstock.

All companies and products mentioned in this book are registered trademarks of their respective owners or developers and are used in this book strictly for editorial purposes; no commercial claim to their use is made by the author or the publisher.

### Library of Congress Cataloging-in-Publication Data

Names: Kroll, Jennifer L., author.
Title: Showdown : animal defenses / Jennifer Kroll.
Description: Huntington Beach, CA : Teacher Created Materials, [2018] | Audience: Grade 4 to 6. | Includes index.
Identifiers: LCCN 2017017375 (print) | LCCN 2017030008 (ebook) | ISBN 9781425853570 (eBook) | ISBN 9781425849832 (pbk.)
Subjects: LCSH: Animal defenses--Juvenile literature.
Classification: LCC QL759 (ebook) | LCC QL759 .K76 2018 (print) | DDC 591.47--dc23
LC record available at https://lccn.loc.gov/2017017375 Library of Congress Cataloging-in-Publication Data

## Teacher Created Materials

5301 Oceanus Drive
Huntington Beach, CA 92649-1030
http://www.tcmpub.com

### ISBN 978-1-4258-4983-2

© 2018 Teacher Created Materials, Inc.

# Table of Contents

# Face Off!

Lions gather at a water hole in Africa. As a rhinoceros steps out of the water, a lioness springs. Her claws grip the rhino's back. But the rhino spins and shakes her off. With its horn lowered, it charges the lions. The lions back away and scatter.

## Getting Defensive

It is dangerous out there! Animals have amazing ways of surviving when faced with a scary showdown. Some creatures, such as rhinos, have powerful bodies and sharp horns. Other animals defend themselves with claws, teeth, or speed.

### All Together Now

Many animals live and work in groups to stay safer. Musk oxen stand side by side in a circle when threatened by wolves or other **predators**. They keep their calves safe in the center of the circle.

## A Quick Escape

The pronghorn uses its speed to escape predators. Pronghorns can run 40 miles (64 kilometers) an hour. That is as fast as cars on the road!

# Armored Animals

It takes thick skin to shake off a lion attack. That is exactly what a rhino has. Its tough skin acts like a suit of armor. Rhino skin can be up to 2 inches (5 centimeters) thick. It is made of layers of collagen. This substance is also found in human skin, bones, and tendons. The collagen layers crisscross each other, making the skin super strong.

Other animals also sport "armor" of some kind. Turtles and tortoises have protective shells. A pangolin is covered in tough scales. It defends itself by curling up into a scaly ball. Armadillos use this same trick to **foil** predators.

### Borrowed Armor

Hermit crabs are not born with shells. Instead, they find and move into abandoned seashells. When they outgrow a shell, they find a bigger one. Hermit crabs carry their shell homes around with them to stay safe.

white rhinoceros

nine-banded armadillo

box turtle

pangolin

## Outback Armor

A falcon circles over the Australian **outback**. It spots a small lizard. It's lunchtime! The falcon swoops. The would-be **prey** is no ordinary lizard. It is a thorny dragon, covered in sharp spikes. Under attack, the lizard puffs up its chest. The falcon decides that this lizard might be too much trouble. The bird flies off to seek its meal elsewhere.

Many lizards have armor-like skin. Thorny dragons are a **striking** example. These Australian reptiles have another cool defense. Each dragon has a spiky, knob-like "false head" on its neck. When it tucks its head down, the false head sticks out. Predators see the false head and the tucked head and think the lizard is larger than it really is.

## Drop It and Run!

Some animals can drop parts of their bodies to escape from a predator. This is called *autotomy* (uh-TAW-tuh-mee). This is the case for dormice, wolf spiders, and geckos. When these animals are under attack, they **sacrifice** something to get away.

### Dormouse

Dormice are relatives of mice and squirrels. The skin on a dormouse's tail is very thin. It can break off easily if a predator grabs it. This allows the dormouse to escape. Afterward, the skinless portion of the tail falls off. The lost tail (or tail section) does not grow back.

## Wolf Spider

All spiders have eight legs, but only some of them can lose legs easily. Wolf spiders hunt without webs. When grabbed by a predator, the legs of these spiders can come off to let them run away. Younger spiders can even regrow the leg they lose.

## Gecko

Geckos' tails are divided into sections. Between each section is a *fracture zone*, an area where the tail can easily break apart. When geckos are in danger, their tails may simply fall off. The dropped tails continue wiggling, which can distract predators. Geckos grow back their lost tails.

# Now You See It

A dark shadow moves through the water above a coral reef. It's a shark! A cuttlefish senses that it is in danger. This small, squid-like creature cannot hope to outpace the much larger predator. The cuttlefish's body begins to change color rapidly. Its skin becomes the same shade as the nearby coral. Its extended arms look like coral branches. The cuttlefish has such good **camouflage** that the shark swims right by.

Cuttlefish are masters of disguise. They can change their appearance at will. This ability helps them escape predators. It also helps them catch prey and impress potential mates.

## Not a True Fish

A cuttlefish is a mollusk, not a fish. A mollusk is an animal with a soft body and no spine. Squid, clams, octopuses, and snails are all mollusks.

# Clever Cuttlefish

Cuttlefish have large brains and are very smart. Scientists have shown that cuttlefish can solve problems and learn maze patterns.

## Blending In

There are a few other animals like cuttlefish. Chameleons, squid, and octopuses can change colors quickly, too.

Many other animals use camouflage for defense. Instead of changing colors, they blend into their environment. Snowshoe hares have white fur in winter. This helps them blend in with the snow. The speckled coats of young white-tailed deer help them stay hidden in the forest.

## "Leaf "Me Alone

A dead leaf floats to the ground, but it flies away before it lands. Surprise! It is actually a living dead-leaf butterfly. Predators needs sharp eyes to spot this insect.

Other insects use the same kind of camouflage. Leaf insects look just like the leaves they eat. Stick insects resemble twigs.

### See a Dragon?

It may look like floating seaweed, but those "weeds" are really a leafy sea dragon. These relatives of sea horses live off the coast of Australia.

snowshoe hare

## Praying Mantis

Praying mantises are insects that have many types of camouflage. Some mantises look like flowers to lure bugs into their clutches. Another mantis species looks a lot like an ant. This keeps it safe from predators that avoid ants.

# DIG DEEPER

## Super Squid Defenses

Like cuttlefish, squid change color to blend in and hide. Here are some of their other amazing defenses.

### An Inky Escape

Inside a squid's body is a sac full of ink. Squid can shoot this ink out through their siphons (SY-fuhns). The ink cloud startles predators. It blocks their view and distracts them, giving the squid time to escape.

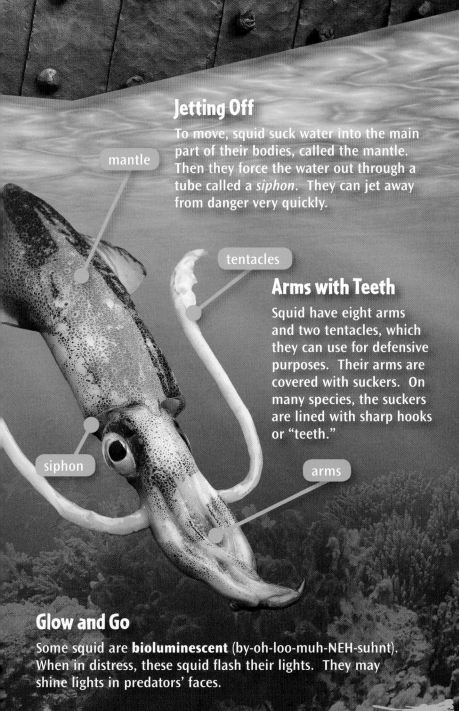

## Jetting Off

To move, squid suck water into the main part of their bodies, called the mantle. Then they force the water out through a tube called a *siphon*. They can jet away from danger very quickly.

mantle

tentacles

## Arms with Teeth

Squid have eight arms and two tentacles, which they can use for defensive purposes. Their arms are covered with suckers. On many species, the suckers are lined with sharp hooks or "teeth."

siphon

arms

## Glow and Go

Some squid are **bioluminescent** (by-oh-loo-muh-NEH-suhnt). When in distress, these squid flash their lights. They may shine lights in predators' faces.

# Keep-Away Spray

A hungry wolf spider spots a bombardier beetle. It moves toward its prey and is ready to pounce.

Bang! A loud sound startles the spider. A boiling spray hits its legs and eyes. The spray not only burns but smells terrible. Bang! The foul spray explodes from the beetle's body again. The wolf spider turns and scurries away.

Bombardier beetles shoot hot, smelly spray out of **glands** in their backsides. The spray is a mixture of two **chemicals**. These are kept in two separate chambers in their bodies. When the beetles sense danger, the chemicals flow together. Mixed together, they heat up and explode!

### Bombs Away

How did the bombardier beetle get its name? Bombardiers were U.S. Air Force members. They dropped bombs from planes during World War II.

## Feeling the Burn

A bombardier beetle's spray is boiling hot. It is more than 212°F (100°C)! The beetle can shoot this spray up to 20 times in a row.

bombardier beetle

# Black-and-White Warning

Who needs armor, speed, or camouflage? Skunks have none of these defenses. Yet they are preyed upon by few animals.

Like bombardier beetles, skunks defend themselves by spraying a stinky liquid. Their spray can travel up to 9.8 feet (3 meters). People can smell this spray from more than a mile away.

Often, though, skunks do not need to spray. Predators see their black and white stripes and know to steer clear. Skunks have what is called a "warning **coloration**."

Striped polecats have the same coloration. These weasel relatives live in Africa. Like skunks, polecats defend themselves with spray that smells horrible!

### Defending the Nest

Green wood hoopoes make a spray that smells like rotten eggs. The birds use the spray around their nest to keep predators away.

# THINK LINK

▶ Can you think of any other animals with a warning coloration? (Hint: It does not have to be black and white.)

▶ Great horned owls often prey on skunks. These predators lack one of the five senses. Can you guess which one?

▶ Skunks prefer to avoid using up their spray. What might a skunk do to avoid spraying?

# Playing Dead

It is dusk, and a Virginia opossum wanders through a clearing. Another animal is looking for dinner, too. The opossum spots a coyote. Danger!

The opossum does not run. Instead, it falls down and "plays dead." Its mouth hangs open, and its **limbs** become stiff. The coyote ignores the "dead" opossum and continues on its way.

Many predators only attack living and moving prey. This is why some animals play dead as a defense. Opossums can keep up the act for hours. To see if the danger has passed, they move their ears to listen for other animals. Once they know they are safe, they get right back to what they were doing.

### Sick Trick

Opossums sometimes fake being sick. They drool and try to look weak and ill. This works because predators tend to avoid sick prey.

# STOP! THINK...

Virginia opossums do not just live in Virginia. This map shows their range. What are some other U.S. states where these opossums live?

## A Snake Fake Out

The eastern hognose snake is another species that plays dead. When frightened, these snakes roll onto their backs with their mouths open. While in this position, they sometimes vomit. It is unclear why the snakes do this. It could be that the sight of the vomit, which could include a poisonous toad or newt, might scare off predators. These snakes are **immune** to the poison. It might be that vomiting lightens their stomachs so the snakes can flee.

Hognose snakes are great actors! Besides playing dead, they have other defenses, too. They can release a foul-smelling fluid from scent glands. They also have mildly **venomous** bites, though the venom is not very dangerous to humans.

### Named for Its Nose

The hognose snake got its name from its nose. Its turned-up nose looks a little like a pig snout. Hognose snakes are nicknamed "puff adders" because they puff themselves up to look fierce.

# Survival

Animals are amazing. They use different defenses to survive. Some stay safe by playing dead. Others have armor-like skin. Some use camouflage to hide from danger. Others blast predators with smelly spray.

Animals in one area may have many ways to protect themselves. Animals in another place may just have a few defenses. This is because they face different dangers.

What natural defenses do humans have? How did our **ancestors** stay safe from predators? These defenses affect our lives now in a different way than in the past. What would you do if you were faced with a sudden, scary showdown?

## A Change of Defense

Many animals use more than one form of defense. They may use these defenses at different times. They may change methods of defense as they go through their life cycles.

caterpillar and monarch butterfly

chameleon
camouflaging

## The Landscape of Escape

Animals choose their home turfs with defense in mind. They select spots that can help keep them safe. Trees, rocks, sand, and water might be used as hiding places or safety zones.

# Glossary

**ancestors**—relatives who lived long ago

**bioluminescent**—able to glow in the dark

**camouflage**—a disguise that allows one to blend in, or the act of blending in

**chemicals**—certain kinds of liquids or gases

**coloration**—patterns or colors on an animal

**foil**—to stop someone's plan

**glands**—parts of the body that release fluids

**immune**—not affected by

**limbs**—a person's or animal's arms, legs, or wings

**outback**—a desert-like part of Australia where few people live

**predators**—animals that hunt for and eat other animals

**prey**—an animal that is hunted and killed for food; to hunt for food

**sacrifice**—to give up something that is valued

**striking**—attracting attention by being remarkable

**venomous**—having a toxic bite or sting

# Index

# Check It Out!

## Books

Grambo, Rebecca. 1997. *Amazing Animals: Defenses*. Kidsbooks, Inc.

Helman, Andrea. 2008. *Hide and Seek: Nature's Best Vanishing Acts*. Walker Childrens.

Kaner, Etta. 1999. *Animal Defenses: How Animals Protect Themselves*. Kids Can Press.

Wilsdon, Christina. 2009. *Animal Defenses*. Chelsea House.

Yaw, Valerie. 2011. *Color-Changing Animals*. Bearport Publishing.

## Video

*Ultimate Wildlife: Animal Defense*. Columbia River Entertainment.

## Websites

PBS. *Wild Kratts*. www.pbskids.org/wildkratts/.

Smithsonian Education. *Here's Looking at You, Squid*. www.smithsonianeducation.org/families/point_click/activitysheets/si_activity_squid.pdf.

# Try It!

What is your favorite animal?  Draw or print out a picture of the animal.  Write a description of it by answering the questions below.  If you do not know the answers, do some research online or in a library.

🐾 Where does this animal live?

🐾 What are its daily habits?

🐾 Which predators pose a threat to this animal?

🐾 What other threats does it face?

🐾 How does the animal stay safe?  What kinds of defenses does it use?

🐾 On your picture, label the parts of the animal that help it defend itself.

# About the Author

Jennifer Kroll is the author of 20 books for kids and teachers. She used to write and edit *Read*, a classroom magazine for students. Kroll likes to learn and write about science. She lives in Connecticut with her husband and two children. Kroll thinks her sense of humor is her best defense. However, she doubts it would help in case of an attack by a humorless polar bear.